Norma Dunning

Eskimo Pie

A Poetics of Inuit Identity

Published by BookLand Press Inc.
15 Allstate Parkway
Suite 600
Markham, Ontario L3R 5B4
www.booklandpress.com

Printed in Canada

Front cover image © Annamareva

Library and Archives Canada Cataloguing in Publication

Title: Eskimo pie : a poetics of Inuit identity / Norma Dunning.
Names: Dunning, Norma, author.
Description: Series statement: Modern indigenous voices series
Identifiers: Canadiana (print) 20200234951 | Canadiana (ebook) 20200234978 | ISBN 9781772311136 (softcover) | ISBN 9781772311143 (EPUB) | ISBN 9781772311150 (PDF)
Classification: LCC PS8607.U5539 E95 2020 | DDC C811/.6—dc23

We acknowledge the support of the Government of Canada through the Canada Book Fund and the support of the Ontario Arts Council, an agency of the Government of Ontario. We also acknowledge the support of the Canada Council for the Arts, which last year invested $153 million to bring the arts to Canadians throughout the country.

Silence is not golden.

To all those who believed I was a poet
before I did. Ma'na.

Table of Contents

An Old Inuit Woman

An old Inuit woman ambles out onto the cool,
morning Tundra
little girls on either side, holding hands as one.
She is the Elder,
they are the learners.
She takes them to the crest of the small hill
where the girls bend to gather twigs.

It is a simple task.

What they bring back will start the fires
boiling the caribou.
What they bring back will feed the embers
on the damp spring nights while others sleep.

The girls run about the hill making tiny piles of sticks
bringing them back to the old woman
whose wrinkled brown hands feel the length
and snap the small willows to an even size.

She feels for how dry they are and wraps them
one by one into a piece of caribou hide.

The little ones scamper on either side of the hill
at the end of their task, the Elder slaps the ground hard.
Two heads turn towards the sound of the shudder.

The girls rush to gather the old woman
helping her stand,
one on each side.
The old woman keeps the bundle of willows
tying it around her crooked back.
She takes a hand from each little girl
And they guide the Elder back to camp.

The old woman is blind
and the girls are deaf.
Together they complete a worthy task.
It is how they maintain their importance to the group.
It is how they keep themselves alive.

Mamaqtuq (Good Tasting or Smelling)

Roll out of my hides
to smell the winds.
Looking every way
for the shadows to
show. Women gather
twigs and moss, kill
kuutsiuti,
the smaller keepers of
small life.
Ilnautuq.
Crawling, sliding along
Taalu,
smelling the winds.

An Eskimo Proclamation

We came here to make you better
Teaching you church and how to knit sweaters

Changed your names and made them right
You dirty little animals full of fight

Taught you how to wash your hands
Took you off your hostile lands

Brought you into our enlightened age
Gave you names on a census page

You're happier than you've ever been
A better side of life you have finally seen

Our mission is soon complete
You will no longer eat raw meat

You'll soldier on in our god's name
You lowly people we have tamed

You will thank us for this soon one day
And on your land, we will forever stay

Inukshuk

it told you where
the water was
the streams of human life
heard the cry of trust filled
tears
it brought comfort
it made you know only
one thing
someone else had been
on this cold desert
before you and
survived
it brought hope
to those lost and
no matter how many people
were with you
it meant that you were not
alone
your mitted hand
strokes its rough edges
and feels the
electric waves of
endurance

Eskimo Pie I

Found on Wikipedia under
"Eskimo Pie"

YEA BO

I should say we do have

ESKIMO PIES

Not only in Vanilla, Chocolate and Strawberry flavor, but in combinations of all flavors.

ESKIMO PIE is a chocolate covered, tin foil wrapped Ice Cream bar that can be eaten like a chocolate candy bar.

Handled at Our
DAIRY STORE

and by our dealers

REICHARDT'S
WHETSTONE'S
RACINE'S
THE ACADEMY

10 Cents

Buy Sidwell's Products for Quality

SIDWELL'S

The Home of Pasteurized Dairy Products

My response to the ad:

YEAH BRO

I should say we do have

ESKIMO LIES
Not only in northern Canada and
Urban centers, but in
combinations of all flavors.
ESKIMO LIES is a sugar covered
Conception of Northern Peoples
Handled at Our
GOVERNMENT OFFICES

And by our general public
LIBERALS,
PC's, RCMP
& THE ACADEMY

NO SENSE
Buy Eskimo Lies - A Quality
PRODUCT OF CANADA
The Home of PASTEURIZED Inuit
History

Kudlik

There is more to this lamp than the lighting of it.
Shared in its shadows are laughter,
Crying, and the tears of so long ago.
The tears of a sickness changing us forever.

Echoes of tuberculosis.

Once we were well, and we gathered *manniq*.
We slept in peace under spring stars.
Hearing our giggles and sighs mixed
Only with the sounds of the earth.

Disease took us from home and away, far away
To stay locked in prisons of white walls.
Coughing up the blood of *puvak* and longing for home.

No more the *qulliq* to warm our spirits, warm our hearts,
Heat our lives, feed our stomachs.
Our revolution came in *Kabloona* Bacteria,
And the light of the *kudlik* grew dim.
Black wisps answered our cries,
Blowing out the wick of what we once were.

Naukkuuqpit (Where Do You Pass Through?)

When I came to this place I had a cough.
It was a red cough and it hurt me.
My bones cried with pain and my heart kept beating.

I didn't understand. How could this be?

When I came to this place, I had to lay in a white bed.
A white bed with white sheets and white lights.
The people were white too, white people in
White dresses or white shirts, they told me words
But I couldn't understand and my heart kept beating.

I could look out the window and see more white people.
White people in black cars, sometimes lots of cars and
Then all the cars would disappear and come back again,
Later in the day.
In this place even the nights are white.

There were other people there who coughed like me
They talked a bit like me,
but they didn't close their words right.
They brought me white food,
Mashed potatoes and hot white soup.
It tasted like nothing, not even snow.

One day, after many days of white nights and lights,
My heart stopped beating and my red cough was still.
Now I lay in this place, under the ground and I know
What's on top of me, but I'm not home.

Itqumilaq (that is how it is)

Reflections on the Charles Camsell Hospital mass burial site in Edmonton, AB. There are twenty-two bodies of Aboriginal children buried in the east garden on the current site. It has never been excavated. The bodies and identities of these children have never been returned home or acknowledged, nor have their families been notified of their deaths. All hospital records from the time of the TB era of the hospital have been destroyed. Five of the children are said to be Inuit (Trotten, S.; Hitchcock, R. 2001, Genocide of Indigenous Peoples*).*

Does This Mean She Never Lived?

Ancestry Dot C A
White people like to do this
It's called genie-ollie-gee

It makes them excited, they tell others
Form groups, set up internet sites, and
Declare themselves a
Soo-sigh-et-tee

Locking themselves away in an archive
Digging deep into a past they may be able to claim
And like a child they shout:
"I found it!"
"I am related to the King of England!"
"My Aunt was a war bride!"
"My Uncle was a pirate!"

She never had a birth certificate.
Does this mean she never lived?

The disc system missed her.
She never got to hang the string around her neck.
She was busy in residential school at the time.

There was no number to replace her name.
Does this mean she wasn't Inuit?

No piece of official Government paper to say
Who or what or when she was.
No disc number to register her breath.

She never had a passport because she never had
a disc number because she never had a birth certificate.

A Stand-Alone Inuk

I've learned this from anaana:
to be who I am without anyone's blessing or nod

I've learned that a plastic card is not what defines an Inuk
no matter where I stand I am only Inuit

I've learned that the language doesn't make me better
or more or less

Many children haven't been taught Inuktitut especially after
your great escapes south on the arms of white men

I won't be accepted inside northern igloo-shaped minds
your social harpoons baited with lateral violence

I speak from what I know
how she taught me be.

Can I be rejected for not being "traditional?"
What does that word mean?

I do not eat muktuk, and remember, our ancestors did not
dip it into Soya Sauce or Ketchup.

Many Inuit have never lived inside the
tundra or hunted seal.

There comes a time, to put all that away
and accept each other with love and understanding.

I am waiting for that time, and for now and perhaps
forever I will remain

A Stand-Alone Inuk

Concrete Eskimo

My toes don't tap the tundra,
they side step city sidewalk cracks instead.
I've never worn a mukluk
to say who I am.
I've never spoke the language
so they all can understand.

My toes don't tap the tundra,
but I am here. I am one of them.
Even if they don't want me to be.
Even if they look at me and wonder,
no you're not, you don't have the features.
Because in everybody's head, there's an idea.
An idea of what an Eskimo looks like
and sounds like and smells like.

My toes don't tap the tundra,
my own people look down
from further north on me and wonder,
no you're not, you don't have the features.
Because in everybody's head there's an idea.
An idea of what an Inuk looks like
and sounds like and smells like.

My toes don't tap the tundra,
but I am what I claim I am,
My mother was one of them and she gave me
them, whether anyone likes it or not.

My toes don't tap the tundra,
They side step on city sidewalk cracks,
And wonder,
if anyone
will ever
accept me
as I am.

Trappers' Wife

(For my Auntie)

It's either silence,
Or wind cracking my body in half.

Wind is the only thing breaking this daily,
drawn out stillness.
The only travelling blast is tucked inside an airstream.

"Barren Lands" they call it.
Completely barren,
Like my womb.

Shrubs shudder and berries bounce
but nothing touches my ankle.

It is only autumn, already the cold is
slicing into the lines of my cheeks.
Icicles dangle from the hairs of my nose
clanging like tiny wind chimes.

Sometimes I shout my husband's name
to break the sound of my own thoughts.

I try to remember we are here
to make our fortune from the tiny white fox
thriving on this echo-filled tundra.

Folks back home wear it.
We are Hudson's Bay Company people.

I ache for the sound of another woman's voice.

Polar Opposites

The green spongy couch sags at one end,
the end where the Inuit Auntie sits.
Her belly button rollercoasters across her kneecaps
like a big marble as
she chuckles beside my mom.

Mirrors of one another, dark hair, slanted black eyes,
skin the colour of soft suntans.
Their heads tip to the same side when they laugh,
but they are different.

My mother is slim.
Her left hand pinches a home-rolled
cigarette, waves of smoke paint nicotine brush stroke
stains against her long, A-shaped nails.

Auntie doesn't smoke.
Her hands are square.
Her fingernails short.
They are talking about what a nuisance ground is.
Auntie says she wants to go there, to see that party
Mom is giggling and telling her it's the dump,
the garbage dump.

Auntie's belly breaks into tsunami waves of laughter,
her marble plopping to the floor.
"I thought it was a place to go make noise," she spits out.
"I thought it was a place to go be a nuisance!"

They look the same at a glance but
Auntie bothers Mommy.
Auntie brings with her all the memories of the north that
are never spoken or shared.

She brings with her bad and sad times.
The convent. Being orphans.
She is the one link to the real world of my Mother.
The world Mommy keeps hidden in glasses
of daily red wine.

They laugh like two old white bear women when they
are together, their eyes crinkle, their heads
sway in unison but inside they are
polar opposites.

My Mother's Tongue

Don't speak it.
Don't talk it
or think it.

Don't say it.
Don't mutter it.
Don't dream in it.
Don't whisper it.
Don't let those words slide
between your lips into your sister's ears.

Don't ever let anyone
hear it.
Keep it inside yourself.
Lock it to your throat.

Never let the words slip out.
The words your mother whispered to you
before you saw the sky.
The words that told you who and what and where
you were.
Now you are here.

Those words are bad words.
They are dirty.
The are ugly.
They mean nothing in this place.
They never will.
The hooded skirts tell you to talk right,
Quit that crying.
Stop those words.
They beat you and beat you
and you know you can't talk it.

Never again.
Get on your knees and ask forgiveness.
Don't speak it.
Don't talk it or think it.

My own mother's language never came to me.
Her first words were taken away
and I can't give them to anyone.
It's not her fault.

Can Ya Speak It?

Fat snowflakes falling from cold grey skies
Melting the burning question filling her eyes
Can ya speak it? Her tongue is hot to ask
I know what's next, she wants to unmask.

The question marking?
My Evidence of being Eskimo.
Only Native peoples need to provide
Plaintive proof that will guide

Being measured by a lingo meter stick
Penned height, and width against a bar
No one else needs to pass this test
A German, a Swede or a winter star.

Eskimo Pie II

(A practical recipe for Inuit people
requiring colonization)

Oh give me a piece of that Eskimo Pie

(Base)
16 crushed chocolate wafers
4 tbsps of melted butter

An entire grouping of humanity
Secured in residential school, left to die
Let me see that chubby little brown face packed

(Filling)
with 32 marshmallows
1/2 cup milk
1/8 tbsp of msg

Smiling inside a fur-ringed padlocked space

Include:
1 tbsp of vanilla and
1 cup of heavy cream – whipped.
Beat the little heathens, put them into their place

Melt the marshmallows, along with their mother tongues
Whiten with milk,
Add salt to the wounds

Put vanilla in a double-boiler
Turn the heat on high
Bring to a boil
Simmer and strain, removing all their relatives

Cool the filling
Fold in the whipped cream
Pour into a pie plate

Slice and Assimilate

(Sufficient for 65,000 Inuit. This recipe can be slightly modified to include First Nations and Métis Canadians).

I Don't Want to Know

I don't want to know what it's like to be Eskimo.

I live in a world of iPods and iPhones,
all my communication is done in text.

I Wear D&G glasses in my high tower apartment
where I can look out over the city.
I got PS1 and PS2, Xbox and I love you Mom,
but I don't want to know what it's like to be Eskimo.

I have street lights and sirens to take me through the night
maybe it isn't right, but…
I don't want to know what it's like to be Eskimo.

Don't talk to me about Angaviadnak,
or Grandma's northern ways.
I got hip hop nonstop and rap to fill my days.

What would it give me to travel back in time?
A big quip, a little sip of tea to warm my spine.

I hear the geese, I look up, I know they're heading north
but I got iPods and iPhones
Hip hop nonstop and rap to fill my days.

They honk down at me, asking me to come along.
But Mom, I got a laptop and a real job and
you don't know what you're talking about.

Because in the end:

I don't want to know what it's like to be Eskimo.

Bunn

Just another Aboriginal kid
dead in Edmonton.
Lying there amongst melting snow and budding trees.
A golf course where white people indulge in expensive
fun and sport.

She's pretty.
Even dead she's pretty.
But she's just another Inuit kid
dying homeless in Edmonton.

Sharing bottles of cheap wine
with her mom.
Sleeping in parking lots and
washing away yesterday with booze,
blurring up tomorrow with an alcoholic haze.

Cops can't sort out who she is.
Put pictures of her hoodie in the Edmonton Journal.
Get a name.
Find a mom who says
she was fine the last time they spooned together on the
concrete.

Papers say "No Foul Play."
An Inuk girl dying on a golf course is normal.
No need to investigate, toxicology reports will explain
this life.

Only nineteen years old but what does it matter?
Just another drunken Inuk,
a female updated version of "Skid Row Eskimo."
Apakark and Takkuruq,
Street versions of Adam and Eve.

Her son taken from her at two days old.
Will he become another Cain?

While the rest of the world puts into practice the
hideous and insidious ways of colonialism,
the greens grow greener.
Buds burst out onto the branches
as her spirit wanders the course
hearing others worry about bogeys, birdies and bunkers.

Written in memory of Kerry Takkiruq, whose body was found on an Edmonton golf course in April of 2011.

You Never Went to Hell on Venials

A hard life lived starting as a babe in the
N.W.T. a simple life then of hunting and
trapping and running and running
and running away from residential school
had to be there for his Dad
to get the government cheques based on the boy's school
official records but the land lured him,
trapped him instead and called his
name over and over and over again until he ran and lived
young and alone but free and happy on a barren,
flat scape at twelve years old

Adventure beckoned go to Alberta make money
party and live the stoned high life
arriving by plane to work the rigs
knowing the government man is going to teach you to
        drive
and take care of big machines you'll get a trade
really be someone when you get back to Tuk
king of the road! nineteen years old

Tried for murder you lousy
homeless drunk all you natives
you're all the same anyways eh
really why can't you all just smarten up
and get over it for god's sake! I didn't put you into that
straight jacket or that fuckin' institution
homeless, my ass-it's your choice you like having
endless blurred nights on Edmonton streets suckin'
        back cherry wine
rockin' those rich old bitches in the back seats of their
        cadillacs

Anthony Apakark Thrasher died in a parking lot in downtown Edmonton in July 1989. The title for this poem is taken from Chapter 1 of his autobiography, Skid Row Eskimo.

St. Norbert's Hair

Pull.
Stretch tight.
Pink comb dipped inside the beer mug.
Wrap the long, coarse black hair into twisted circles.

Like cinching a saddle to a horse.
Knee up under the shoulder
Butt the air out of horse's lung.
It exhales,
Haul hard and fast
Yanking the buckle stiff.
It inhales.
The saddle sits rigid and tight.

Mama wets her pointed nails,
Flitting the stray strands of their manes
And fastening them to the sides of their heads.
Bound tightly into thick, brown elastics.
Dead weight braids
Hang from their sagging shoulders.

Black ropes are scooped tight against their heads.
Their eyes more slanted then normal.
Jerking pupils tell me I'm lucky to have the short
Pixie cut.

I'm jealous.
I long for long hair.

I want the tight intu'dlit braids Mama calls "French."

Mama wets the pink comb and
Gently weaves the soggy plastic teeth around my head,
Purring to me about the "wave" in my hair as she
draws circles.

Years later I find pictures of her residential school
online.
I sit in my living room wondering
Why did she give me St. Norbert's hair?

The Token Eskimo Interview

HELP WANTED!
RATE OF PAY: $20/HR
MONDAY – FRIDAY 8 AM - 4 PM
JOB TITLE: ?

EMPLOYER: We are an Inuit owned and operated company!
INUK: Hmm, hmm.

EMPLOYER: We subcontract to all the diamond mines in Nunavut!
INUK: Hmm, hmm.

EMPLOYER: We've been acknowledged for the last two consecutive years for employing the most Aboriginal people in Canada!
INUK: Hmm, hmm.

EMPLOYER: We don't have any Aboriginal people in our Edmonton office.
INUK: Hmm, hmm.

EMPLOYER: Do you speak Inuktitut?
INUK: No.

EMPLOYER: Have you ever been to Nunavut?
INUK: No.

EMPLOYER: Do you read Inuktitut?
INUK: No.

EMPLOYER: We need someone who can translate for us.
INUK: Hmm, hmm.

EMPLOYER: Do you know someone who could?
INUK: Yes. Could I ask what the job is?

EMPLOYER: Hm, hmm, ah, varied.
INUK: Varied? What does that mean?

INUK: You need an Eskimo?
EMPLOYER: Well…

INUK: You need an Inuit person on staff?
EMPLOYER: In a sense…we…

INUK: How much was it an hour?
EMPLOYER: Negotiable!

The Office

sitting in the swivel chair
ergonomic keys laying spread eagled

the click, click, clicking
of keyboards, spelling out the words
the words of nothing
clicking and clacking about stuff

stuff that never goes anywhere for anyone

get up each day and put on those
fancy pressed pants
ride the train, sit in the cubicle
and sit, sit, sit

clickity-clacking

"Aboriginal Affairs and Northern Development Canada"
spelling out the words of nothing
like invisible ink
all the sorrys for this and that
oops, invisible ink spills onto the white pages
the white pages containing the phone book list
of all those Native people who
were fucked right up

fucked right over
fuckin' rights
Native rights written with invisible ink
on white 8.5 by 11-inch bond paper.

Where's the printer?

The Young Fools

(Response to Larkin's *The Old Fools*)

Wearing skinny pants and buckle up boots
Ass crack hanging low. What makes them dress this
 way?
Saying 'LIKE' on repeat, sloppy English suits
Your shoddy way of communicating to the world.
Text. Snap an Instagram. Think you've saved today.
iPhone you love best and Facebook-your only friend
Where is reverence? The heeding of Elder's words
 twirled
For you to sort out and help make sense of time.
"STOP" is empty, you only know to hit "SEND"
Listening to words by dimming fires bores you
No ringtones or waiting messages, it's a crime
 Don't they have a clue?

In this life, you will not know what the moon speaks
Telling us of rain or snow and when to fish
You are blind to the curled leaf, don't know what it
 seeks
On blazing summer days, the iPhone8 won't put food
Onto a plate or whisper to the stars a wish
There's no app for that, there's no app for clouds or
 wind
You will not carry our creation stories-it's crude
Remembering the story of your anaana
It isn't written on a screen to ease your mind.
It can't be true if Google can't search and find it.
No food from heaven, memory is not manna
 Device off – for a bit?

Perhaps youth lacks the time to reminisce.
Recalling waits for the over-thirty crowd.
Is tradition yet something else without bliss?
Instant satisfaction can't be had in old stories.
YouTube has it all, the full truth videoed loud
And spread across the globe, amateur first-hunt tales
No grannies talking over tea with bannocked mores
It's new, live, and direct on a lighted board
Not on trodden moss dotted with blueberry trails
Not on trap lines speckled with large pad prints
Of howling husky barks mixed in with guitar chords
          Life is cyber stints.

No concept of how time tunnels past us
And it becomes too late to hear the Elder's words.
More exciting the daily grind, life kept by a bus
Schedule, eras tick-talk the clock on the phone face
Not the wrist, no moments marked by migrating birds.
Seasons are lost on the young, the truth of the past
Splits into empty black holes, looms the long-ago chase.
The trust that somewhere, some bending soul will stoop
To pick up the words and bring back to the people
The memory of what was and is, make it last
In the first spoken form, stirring spiritual soup
          Hope is here not past.

South of It

I grew up in the north
but not in the north north
other Canadians would call it north.
Not Inuit though.

Every summer we were camping.
My father was transferred
by the military
every second year.

He was a good hunter and
our main food was land food.
From the land we were living on.
Moose, deer, and caribou.

Berry picking was a seasonal event.
Blueberries, and Saskatoon berries were
turned into jams, jellies and pies.
Fish filled the freezer each year.

This was how we lived
but we were not in Nunavut.
We were south of it.

Relatives

It was the season when we would hear the sounds of each other. Sounds that we didn't normally get to hear. Soft summer winds mixed with his snoring. Every one of us getting up through the night to use the ceramic potty. Giggling under old quilts and for once the Department of National Defense sheets weren't with us. It was the sound of freedom. Freedom from clocks and school and books. I don't have to wear shoes again until the first day of school. It was also, freedom from booze.

He didn't get drunk for that one season each year. We were a family during those days. Hot days with gravel roads sending small dust particles into the old station wagon. Dust that would layer itself onto our skin on top of the dirt that was already there. We smelled of campfires and sweat. We ran around in the woods barefoot, and threw rocks into streams, rivers, and oceans.

It was the time when after supper each night we would have only an old wooden bat and an Indian Rubber Ball. He would hit that ball to us and we'd scramble to catch it - gloveless.

Twap! The tiny black ball would be coming towards us like a meteorite and he would shout out how much it was worth. "One hundred!" he'd shout.

We'd scramble like jack rabbits, zigzagging our way to that ball, pushing each other over and laughing. The ball would smack into our palms and no matter how much it hurt we never cried out. We were proud of our bruised palms and at the end of each night we would show off our purple and red polka dot hands to each other before closing our eyes. The sun would melt into the horizon and he would play with us until none of us could see the ball anymore. Days of sitting in a sweaty old station wagon and nights of Indian rubber and fires. We all knew one thing: Soon we'd have to visit those people.

Each summer our freedom was interrupted. His people, very white people, and farmers who kept spotless houses and tight routines. He was the youngest of his four brothers and three sisters and he would arrive with his dirty little band of dark children. I am sure he was pitied by them, the white Presbyterian side. My Dad with his murky-coloured kids and her. She would have been a big, black smudge on a family of blue eyes and strawberry blonde hair. None of them liked her. We knew it. We didn't like them.

Dad missed farming, it was how he was raised. Summer was his time to get back to his roots. This part of summer was a time of hand washing and staying quiet in reformed Christian homes. All six of his children worked Aunts and Uncles' farms. We stayed in our tiny trailer, parked away from the farmhouse. Distance told us where we stood with these people. Long, hot, summer days working other peoples' gardens and fields and wishing for September to fall onto a calendar page.

One Uncle and Aunt were the only people I ever knew who kept their living room wrapped in heavy plastic. It covered everything. When we would visit we would be the savage, dirty children who had to spend our time outside. Allowed in for meals only and our feet under the table after having scrubbed our hands the way surgeons do. We were never allowed to talk at the dining room table. Aunt only wanted to look at us. She invited me one night to visit her alone.

I am sitting on the heavy plastic. It is like visiting the Queen, being ushered into a room that none us were able to be a part of and sitting on a chair that made sweat slide down the crack of your ass. Aunt has a box on her lap. She is giving me a recitation of her poetry. Words that rhyme and bore me.

I can't figure out why I am alone with her and I am uncomfortable. I am wishing for my Mom to come join us. Aunt reads a sampling of her work and then begins to read mine. I am shocked. I didn't know my Mom was sending my poetry off in letters to anyone. Her British accent makes my words sound strange, and foreign. I say not one word. I only want this to end.

Aunt pulls her glasses off from the tip of her nose and says, "You must continue to do this. You have a gift. It's important that someone write about the history of the family." I nod and ask to leave the room. Disappointment shrugs off her tiny body. Savage children never understand anything properly. I meet my mother in the farmyard.

Mom is taking a break from life with a home-rolled cigarette. We look at each other. We grin, both of us try to squish the laughter that is bubbling inside of us. Like naughty children we both look the other way. We say not one word.

I would long to leave the farms and go back to our travelling routine. The routine of cooking over campfires and wearing bruised palms like badges of courage. I longed for the bat and ball and his calling out "One hundred" as we pushed each other over trying to catch the black dot dropping from the sky.

Ataatattiaq Mitsilik
(Grandpa, Who Is Truth)

I'm trying to put it together in my head
Where it all started, how he met her,
And then her and then her.
Did he love any of them?
Did he love all of them?

Brother talks like he knows
but he doesn't.
He knows what the old trappers say but
they never talked about her and her and her.
They talk about him.

He was tough and small and laughed.
He talked it, lived it, ate it and slept it.
At night he fucked it.
Her and her and her.
They made babies,
a girl and a girl and a girl.

Did they love him?
One died.
One was traded off.
One grew older next to him.
Was there any love inside of any of them?

Silenced Once
Recolonization Part I

I spent six weeks in a poetry class, with a globally renowned poet. The following pages recount that journey. I was the oldest student. I was also the only Aboriginal student in the class.

September 6
La Rose Warnings

The do's and don'ts - no water, no coffee, no this or
    that
La Rose sounds like a villain
Ready to spring on each of us and Pounce us into the
    reality of Poetry
"Terrific" - you've used La Rose's word…as though
    any one person
can own any one word
Mental note, "never use 'terrific' again…"
You'll be expected to memorize
Visions of my Grade 5 teacher Mrs. MacDonald
Yardstick clenched in her tiny square fist, slapping
    the backs of my knees
With centimeters, inches and meters as we stood up
    one by one
Next to the hard, wooden desks and recited back to
    her our weekly poems
Hard sharp stinging slaps thwacking the inside of soft
    knee tissue issued
each time we made an error.
La Rose standing next to me with a meter stick pops
    into my head

I lay in bed that night thinking of Robert Frost and all
the miles
he had to go before he could sleep.

Warning of the master of Masters arriving–what to
expect,
to do, others have told me La Rose tries to out Brit the
British
and can a person really take a student for a slave?
What kind of mind thinks like this?
I read the early work by La Rose,
the N-word was in use.
I loved it.
Loved that La Rose talked that way.
Said it straight up.
Now Black La Rose writes about the soft seawater
softness.
What happened to her?

September 11
La Rose - Day 1

I sat in a dentist chair, receiving my first root canal while the world shut down airports and the skies emptied to the silence of terror. I am back in the dentist chair before my first class with La Rose, watching country music videos on a screen too close to my chin. While picks and axes enter my mouth and remove dirt that has moved into the grooves of my gums, I wonder why fire is used so much in each music video while guitars twang and girls cry. Do the images of over a decade no longer matter?

The hygienist speaks of the new house she and her new husband are building and I try to converse while my enamel is under construction. "Ughs" and "ohs" jump downwards from my mouth, jackhammers remove grit and sirens spin in my brain, speaking of the pain of this procedure. Can this day get any better?

The drive to class is filled with sips of water swooshing around my new, shiny teeth, while acrid saliva mixes itself with the smoke from a cigarette. I worry about being tardy, a word that is rarely used anymore but should be because it sounds fun. Words get replaced, updated, displaced, re-made and relocated but in the end tardy is still late. Isn't it?

La Rose is seated, scarf purring about her neck. She looks suave just like her photos. Some age with grace. I wait for the wisdom to spill over onto the table, the wisdom of a craftswoman who has worked hard and long and now dabbles only in the apprenticing of others as a sidebar to writing. I am in a state of awe.

The words arrive: "There's no long ago in poetry. Everything is in the present." I have to remove all those visions of the old guys, the classics and classicals, running up hill and down dale with quills in hand. I have to update the image. Remake them into today with iPads and free verse. History blends into the colours of technology and relocates itself somewhere inside of me. Jumbled and bumbled and broken into a new kind of song Hardy sings to me a rousing song of mourning.

September 13
A Buffet of La Rose

We are all amazed that she speaks to us or reads to us or recites to us and then reads our words. If I was an accomplished eighty something poet would I lay out a buffet of wisdom to such young people?

A buffet of La Rose's words echoes and stays with me. Why have I never tasted this before?

Thomas is not afraid of bravery and he was heroic.

He died in the war. He had returned to it.

Perhaps is not certain.

For Thomas, there is doubt, hesitancy,

he writes as an honest poet.

He examines each tension.

The radiance is slow.

The poem is talking to the poet.

There is a delicate balance between articulation and artifice.

Respect the edges.

Most importantly: If you believe in your words – they have a great force.

September 18
More on Thomas

The eyes of the Master zoom into Thomas. What is the intent of the poet? Why do we analyze these dead guys? How easy it is to say that something is "this" when the writer is not around to tell us it is "that." Cynicism begins to creep into my consciousness. I begin to question La Rose.

She is the Elder Master, but I doubt her interpretation, the minute detail that she interprets for us. Dead poets cannot speak beyond the grave, but I love to hear the Elder Master, to see words through her eyes. To understand the meaning of breath and pause. This is her magic. The Elder Master looks deeper into words. If we were all standing in a field, the sunlight would hit her first.

But, I am the oldest person in the class. On the first day, we were alone for ten minutes. La Rose asked, "Are you the professor?" I replied, "No, I am a student." Her face showed disdain. She didn't like having an older student in the room. She didn't like having a grown up sitting in the chair at the end of the long table. Directly in her line of vision. On day one, she began to ignore me. Speaking left. Speaking right. Never speaking to me. Her eyes never fell in my direction.

I feel all this in our first class, but I try to ignore it. The sense of being silenced grows with each passing second. One hundred and eighty minutes later, I know that my presence is unwelcomed. I know that my age is unwelcomed. I know that my Inuitness is upsetting for her.

If we were all standing in a field, the sunlight would never hit me. La Rose would stand in its way.

September 27
Belittle, Beguile

I am so angry – I can't speak or think
Has Elder Master lost her humanity today?
My words are swill spinning in a filthy kitchen sink
Inuk truth is merely child's play.

"Poetry has no room for pain!"

She knows what residential schools did
Behind locked doors and walls.
My Mom was only a kid.
Elder Master ignores it all.

La Rose removes the subject of my words
And points out a misspoken line
Treating my words like some off-coloured joke

"I hate these foreign words–take them out!"
Inuktitut is indigenous to me, not to her
"Write only in one language! Don't be a moke!"
Inuktitut is not allowed.
I am the donkey in the room.

Form on paper suddenly matters
The room is hushed.
Silence is cracked with chatter
Move a word there, take this line out, broken is my
    will
To tell the truth, the only truth, to the Elder Master
    it is swill

Respect will stay
Because it should
In my heart,
Hard feelings lay
But like my mother, I'll be good
Soon Elder Master will go away.

October 2
Denied & Dismissed

What's worse? Being put under a spotlight or being
dismissed
in silence? What plays inside her white-haired-head
    when I read?

Is she considering what to eat for lunch, or
whether or not to nap
in the sun's dim in after-lunch glow?

She muses aloud,
"What have I done to get so much respect?"
I think: "How do you know you have it?"

Today my words are placed aside
without a groan or a grunt or even a quiet yawn.

My words waft wearily through the air from her
square hand
And are placed silently onto the pile
of "The-Already-Read and Commented-Upon."
Today my words receive no verbal mention
We all see La Rose's physical gesture
Of silencing me.

The other students sit like pigeons on a power line,
Not knowing what they are to do next,
So they do nothing at all.

Not one emotion,
Not one body gesture,
Not one nod.
My words are muzzled.

It's like being 'on hold' for a very long time and hearing
the soft click signaling the end of a call.

It is good my classmates see her as a Poetic Goddess.
They don't acknowledge what is before them.
They stay on the pigeon line.
They are complicit.
In our second to last class
She made sure that I was second class

Last class

La Rose made the grand gesture of taking
her admirers out for lunch for last class.
I learned two things with La Rose.
To upset the Elder Master:
Number one: Show up to class.
Number two: Continue breathing.
But on the last day,
I could not bear to watch her eat.

Years later

I text my son:
La Rose died today!
Best Valentine's Day EVER!! Xo

Silenced Twice
Recolonization Part II

Unpublished

I lay here in the womb of the unpublished
Sloshing around in the amniotic fluid of anonymity

I have been told for three years
That I am emerging

A contradiction containing not one contract
The publishers' birth canal remains undilalated

The rejections are many
Small publishing houses understaffed, over-worked

"We have no time for poetry"
"Interesting work, needs honing"

Other writers chanting
"I ah would ah like to see you ah, ah, ah, whew,
　　　　published"
As the contractions of birthing press hard against me

I have those days
The days of hearing the pants of others

Pushing my words forward
Out into the world
While I fight hard to stay back
Inside the unpublished womb

It's safe in here
No one to tell me I'm wrong
No one to say that I'm a fake
No one to listen to but myself

When I do send my words
Away to a publishing house
I kiss the envelope good bye
And whisper them well

Telling them that I'll always be here
Waiting for them to come back

Rejected and dejected

I remind them they will always be mine
No matter what the rest of the world thinks

I'll swaddle them back to me
Wrapped in soft baby flannel

Rocking them close to my breast
Singing to them in whispered tones

This is the world of the unpublished
The ones who wait

For the nod from the doctors of publishing
Slapping my words once on the bum

While holding the manuscript
Upside down and proclaiming,

"It's a hit!"

And it happened. "The Hit" is published. All the years of writing and rewriting. All the years of keeping her close to me. My manuscript. My girl. No one would ever love her better than me. No one would ever understand her better than me. No one would ever keep her safer than I could. I adore her. I always will.

But I let her go out into the world, inside the brown envelope. I kissed her at the post office. I said, "Have fun girls." I shoved them through the mail slot. Another kind of birthing. I worried about them. How were they? Not one word back from the publisher. Not one whisper. I wait until a year flutters past. I send an email. Yes, they had her, and all the other girls. A communication error. They hand her off to The Readers. The Readers love them all. You have a hit!

The editing, the rewriting of rewrites. The copy/editing the rewriting of the rewriting of the rewrites. The layout. The cover jacket design. The picture of me that I hate on the inside flap. The talking and talking and talking and away she goes to the printer. She's isn't the idea that I had of her in my head. She is misconceived.

I think about her coming to life in print. She won't be only mine anymore. I often stand on the balcony and stare into the night stars. I worry about her. I smoke far too may cigarettes. She'll belong to everybody. She won't be my girl only. The girl who lived inside of me for decades. The girl I carried.

I receive the call from the publisher. She's here! Come and see her. I don't want to. Not immediately. I stay away. Will we know each other any more? Will we recognize each other? Will we disappoint one another?

I wait and think about how she will feel in my hands. I hesitate to celebrate my baby who has entered this world.

I blubber when I finally hold her, like I did with each of my sons. I turn her over and over. I run my hands down her front and back. I stare at her perfection. I love her. I want to protect her. I am so afraid of what this world will do to her, like I was with each of my sons.

It all begins. The launches. The first, the second, the third. Reading and talking and liking that others can like her too. I travel with and for her. I have memorized the parts that were hardest to write. The hardest truths. I practice and practice before each reading. She is lovely.

The glow of a long and happy birth can not linger.
They want surgery done.
I have given birth to an anomaly.
She is sliced.
She is diced.
It's all done quietly and quickly.
I am told I will receive her in a new form.
The imperfection has been removed.
She will look the same only slimmer.
No one needs to know.
It's over.
It's early winter.
It's Abortion.

Remembrance Day

Today we pause
For those who
Kept us here
Our ancestors from long ago

Standing next to us
At cenotaphs
We will think of what they could have been
Each of us with Dad's who fought

To keep us all here
Our Fathers came home
We honour them with 60 seconds of silence

We honour them more
By fighting for what is right
By fighting to stay free
From those who bind us

With rules, and laws
Erasing our right to speak
Or write anything
Fiction or non

Silencing arrives in more democratic forms

Bullets are less visible
Pain is the same
The tomb of the unknown writer
Guarded by John Doe

Is gagging equal to death?

Family and a select few are amazed at the results of my babys' small life. Less then five months old, and they are smothering her slowly.

I run to the westward ocean, to the city on the island. It snows on Christmas Day. The town rejoices. I think about how good it is to be away from harm. I think about how good it is to not be watched. The only thing I have to be is a stranger.

December 29

Delayed and delayed and delayed.
sitting at the airport thinking

about how other people can sleep
in public and not be bothered by

passerby's who glance their way.
I think about how they should

put this on a resume as a skill
"I can sleep publicly!"

Home. Three hours later
then scheduled and trying
to thaw chili for supper

I had sat next to an elder Elder
who told me she came to Canada
from Norway in 1949
with her husband who has since passed.

She asks where I am from.
I say, "I've lived in Edmonton for twenty-seven years."
She seems confused, and asks
again, "But where are you from?"

I tell her that I am Inuit.
Her head nods close to
my mouth,
motioning for me to repeat.
I do again
And again.

I finally yell, "I'm Eskimo!"
A word the elder immigrant understands.

"Oh," she says, "I wondered…
Because you're so dark, and
Your complexion is beautiful.
I thought you were Spanish."

I smile at her thinking of how
The word "Eskimo" can still
make sense in Canada

I lean my head back and close my eyes.

She had looked so disappointed.
I'm so spent.
So tired.
So sick of being kind.

I as so sick of being kind.
I am so sick of being silenced.
I am ready to protect my girl the same way I did my sons.
I am ready to take on the white wolves.
I am ready to speak.
I am ready to watch them squirm.
It's time.

It's time for the world to know that we can no longer silence writers. It's time for the world to know that you can not and do not control creativity. It's time for the white wolves to step away from a cause they do not own. They do not share. A creation of their own imaginations.

The people I trusted have scattered. The people I trusted have vanished. There is no one. There is me. There is her. There is only us. Alone.

This is a long battle.

I think of only one thing as I sit through this mess:
"Instead of being irritated by what writers say, and accusing them of trying to create disturbances which they only describe and announce, it would be better to listen more attentively and take their warnings more seriously." Albert Memmi, Paris, 1965, *The Colonizer and the Colonized.*

Tainna (The Unseen Ones)

I am a southern born and raised Inuk woman. I am not fluent in Inuktitut. I was not raised on raw meat. I have never been to Nunavut, or to my ancestral community of Whale Cove. I was raised in a silent form of Aboriginality. Hushed Aboriginality thrived in my home during my growing up years. Being Inuk was not a topic up for discussion. I do not say that with anger. I say it, because I think that many Aboriginal children grow up this way still. I only knew one thing when I was a little girl. I only knew that I wasn't white.

I remember coming into the house on a sweaty Saturday summer afternoon. We were living on a small military base. My Mom was cutting up potatoes to make French fries. The smell of hot grease filled up the house. I stood behind her and asked, "Mom, what are we?" She turned around startled. She bent down, and pointed her right index finger close to my face and asked, "Why?" When that finger was in use, she meant serious business.

I told her that all the other kids on the playground were talking about being Irish, or Swedish, and how their families came from far away. I will never forget her telling me, "You tell them all you're French! You were born in Quebec, and that's all they need to know!" I did as directed well into my teens.

That memory stays with me, because it is so unlike who my Mom was. My mother was an Inuit woman. Small built, clever hands, and always a laugh or a smile on her face. She had lived her early years in the Keewatin district of northern Manitoba. What she passed onto me were her Padlei Inuit ways of knowing and being. This is not something taught inside a schoolhouse. When she was a little girl, she and her two sisters managed to survive eight full years in a residential school located outside of Winnipeg. It was too costly to send northern children home for the summer.

One of my Aunties' was labelled, 'untrainable,' and was sent to a mental asylum. In time, she was released, and spent a quiet life working in the laundry of a Winnipeg hospital. She never married. She never had children. My other Auntie is the last member standing from my Mom's family. She is ninety-six years old. She married and lived the life of a trapper's wife.

She is the one who would come to visit us. She is the one who would talk about all the things we did not. She is the one who brought up the past. The nuns, the school, their life before, "the convent." She is the one who broke the silence. At age sixteen she confirmed what I was. At age sixteen I knew I was Inuit. I never admitted it to anyone outside of my house.

Inside of my growing up years were many silences, not only of being Inuk but we also never spoke of the domestic abuse or the alcoholism that raged inside of each military house that we lived in. It took me many years to sort it all out. How we were never told what we were. How we only visited my Dad's farming family. How his brothers and sisters often treated us like dirty little savages. The dark-haired, dark-eyed children who had to wash their hands over and over again.

My parents valued education even though their own opportunities had been limited. It was important that each of us kids finished grade twelve, but university was never presented as an option. I believe that the mentality of completing grade twelve only continues with many Inuit families. It is amazing to me that any Inuit people complete a university degree.

For myself, I never thought I would attend university. I am the mother of three grown sons and four grandchildren. My sons' growing up years were spent in Edmonton Housing. When my boys and I came to Edmonton twenty-seven years ago, it was the place that social services put us. I had thought I could work our way out of there within four years, but it took twice as long. The first two years in Edmonton we were a welfare family. I worked so hard at keeping our townhouse clean. I worked hard at washing and ironing all my boys' clothes. I did not want them to look like they were on welfare, even though our address told their schools that we were.

I was like my Mom, in that I never let them identify as Inuit while they were in school. We were Edmonton Housing people, and there would be no further layering of what they were according to a school system. They would not be segregated. They would not be coded as Aboriginal students. We were already in the cycle of poverty, but we didn't have to look it, or allow anyone to classify us further. I began cleaning at night and during the day for various companies and families. They paid in cash. The welfare people never had to know about that income. Eventually I landed a job as a warehouseman, and in time I was working in the company office. We finally moved out of Edmonton Housing.

I begin to learn how to transport freight around the world. I spend the next seventeen years as a logistician with three different globally-based companies. When my sons graduated from high school, I told them that they must now begin to identify as Inuit. It was hard for them, because they were never allowed to previously. They followed through, and it wasn't until they each left home that I allowed them to carry their Nunavut beneficiary cards in their wallets. Their beneficiary cards became their parting gift from me.

I will say that I write a great deal about Inuit identity. Are you Inuit if you are not raised on the tundra? Are you Inuit if you do not speak Inuktitut? Are you Inuit if you don't eat the traditional land food that is not available to you in the south? I write about how I have been measured as an Inuk. I write about how this has affected me. I write about the other Inuit who have also worked at surviving in the southern areas of Canada. I write about the strength we have each gathered because of where we live.

I think of the Inuit babies who lie within their Mothers' bellies now, and in the future. I want them to know that they are Inuit no matter where they stand. I want them to be fearless and confident. My writing is dedicated to all southern Inuit Canadians.

Inuttigut We the Inuit – we are here.

GLOSSARY

Anaana: mother.

Ataatattiaq: Grandfather.

Illnautuq: Caribou looking.

Inukshuk: a structure of rough stones stacked in the form of a human figure.

Itqumilaq: that is how it is.

Kabloona: non-Inuit person.

Kudlik: crescent-shaped oil lamp carved from stone.

Kuutsiut: iver bird, smaller than ptarmigan.

Manniq: wick of moss.

Mitsilik: who is truth.

Naukkunqpit: where do you pass?

Puvak: lung.

Qulliq: stone lamp.

www.ingramcontent.com/pod-product-compliance
Ingram Content Group UK Ltd.
Pitfield, Milton Keynes, MK11 3LW, UK
UKHW062308290726
14090UKWH00018B/944